I HEARD A
SCREAM
IN THE STREET

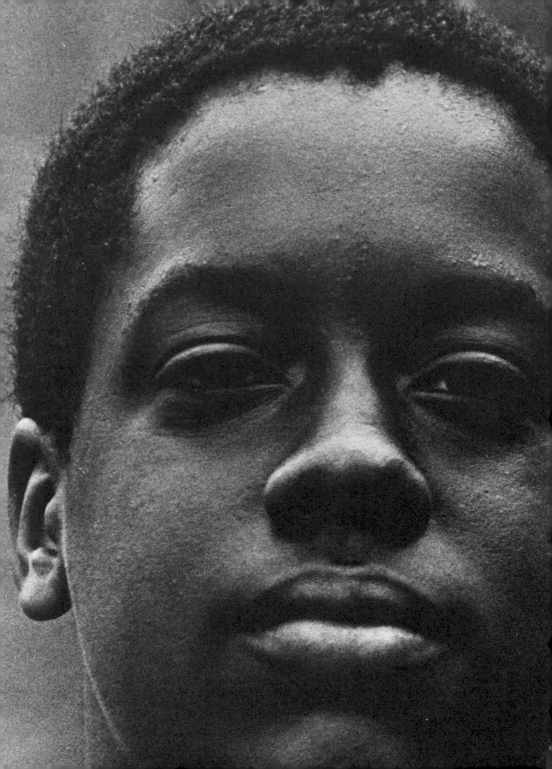

I HEARD A

SCREAM

IN THE STREET

Poems by Young People in the City

Illustrated with Photographs by Students

SELECTED BY NANCY LARRICK

Published by M. Evans and Company, Inc, New York

and distributed in association with

J. B. Lippincott Company, *Philadelphia and New York*

Thanks are due to the following authors, publishers, publications and agents for permission to use the material included:

Paul M. Christensen for "Scribbled on a once-clean wall . . ."

Vernon L. Davey Junior High School, East Orange, New Jersey, for "Faces" by Shelley McCoy and "Why Do They Stare?" by Wendy Rountree, with authors' permission.

Michael Deighan for "Beneath the aging buildings . . ."

ECLECTIC National Student Literary Magazine, 1208 East Clivedon Street, Philadelphia, Pa., No. 2, Spring, 1969, for "A Scream" and "A War Game" by Allan Richards, "What's in the Newspaper Tonight?" by Ron Holzinger, "Neighborhood" by Gwynne L. Isaacs. Reprinted by permission of ECLECTIC.

Denise Embry for "The Thoughts of a Child"

Extended Day Enrichment Class in Creative Writing, Beverly Hills Unified School District, Beverly Hills, California, for "Zoo" by Anna Boorstin.

FLAMINGO, 1969, McClymonds High School, Oakland, California, for "Sleeping Beauty" by Charles Johnson, "Will the Wig Be Big Enough?" by Peggy Crawford, "Watch Dog" and "Jail" by Tim Barnes, and FLAMINGO, 1970, for "The City is Burning" by Henry A. Lewis, and "Ghetto" by Roger Johnson, with authors' permission.

I.S. 55, Brooklyn, New York, for "You shout about freedom . . ." by Wilburt, "But I'm Still a Nigger" by Nathaniel, "Me" by Danny, and "No One" by Barbara.

Howard Jones for "No Chains"

LIKE IT IS, No. 2, a class magazine, English Department, Haaren High School, New York, New York, for "Crowds on the train . . ." by Henry Gibau and "From my window . . ." by Alonzo Dunlap.

Reginald Lockett for "Haiku"

Lorenza Loflin II for "A Black Man's World"

Stella Mancillas for "Who Am I?"

Cathy Magee for "A Street Is a River"

Lucia Martin for "What Now?"

Stephen T. Mather High School, Chicago, Illinois, for "Subway Ride on a Summer Day" by Debbie Solomon, "I wanted badly to write . . ." by Neal Rosner, "I stand here against this lamp post" by Ron Chafetz, "The Generation Gap" by Ellen Alexander, "The Last Empty Seat" by Richard Goodkin, "Free at Last" by Arthur Alenik; as published in HORIZON, 1968, with authors' permission.

George Meade, National Process Workshop for Teachers and Writers Collaborative, for "Nature Poem"

MIRACLES AND MIRAGES, Havenscourt Junior High School, Oakland, California, for "The Lonesome Boy" by Vicki White.

Oakland Technical High School, Oakland, California, for "i have friends . . ." by Cheryl Thornton.

Aries Paige for "Have you ever loved . . ."

POETRY SEARCH ANTHOLOGY, Center for Urban Education, Fordham University, for "Houses bent over look like . . ." by Ricky McBride, "The World Has Changed" by Charlotte Liberty Walker, "Summer in the City" by Daniel McNally, "The swings in the park . . ." by Cathleen McGlynn.

Rosati-Kain High School, St. Louis, Missouri, for "City Child" by Eileen McCormick.

Scholastic Magazines, Inc., for "SITTING UPON THE PICASSO KOALA BEAR . . ." by James Tomasello, with author's permission. For "love apple" by Martha Scheiner, reprinted from SCHOLASTIC SCOPE, copyright © 1967 by Scholastic Magazines, Inc., with permission of publisher.

SPECTRUM, 1968, Huntsville High School, Huntsville, Alabama, for "Why Do They?" by Betty Wilkinson and "Alone" by Mary Jane Hiers.

Student Nonviolent Coordinating Committee for "Mine" by Alice Jackson

THIS IS JUST TO SAY, Goucher College Poetry Project, Florence Howe, Director, for "She came with lips of brown" by Betti Cox, "My Black Boy" by Carla Wade, "This Is a Black Room" by Joshua Beasley, and "Response to 'This Is a Black Room'" by Deborah Dixon, with authors' permission.

Mary A. Tobin, Jamaica Plain, Massachusetts, for "What Is a City?"

Trustees of the Public Library of the City of Boston for "Run, Child, Run Fast" by Carol Williams, "I Have No Fears" by Joy Silverstein, "Nobody Collects the Papers" by Linda Warren and Donna Dickson, "Window; 3rd Story; 5th to the Right, Morning" by Roger L. Drapeau, Jr., as published in WHAT IS A CITY?

Voice of the Children, Inc. copyright © VOICE OF THE CHILDREN, INC. 1969 for "i am frightened that . . .", "Odyssey of a Slum," and "Escape the Ghettos of New York" by Vanessa Howard; "beer cans . . ." by Michael Goode, and copyright © 1968 VOICE OF THE CHILDREN, INC. for "The City" by Juanita Bryant; with authors' permission.

WHAT'S HAPPENING MAGAZINE, Inc., Teachers College, Columbia University, for "This Place" by Conrad Graves, "WALK TALL MY BLACK CHILDREN" by Sharón Boone, "Yes, I Am a Negro" by John West, "Harlem 1960 & 1968" by Pauline Bird, "Walking past small and dingy cafés" and "Boys Don't Cry" by Lydia Martinez,

3

"Walk Down My Street" by Vincent Dorsett, "Social Comment" by Lawrence Fishberg, "Hard But Soft" by William Barbour, Jr.

Yale Alumni Magazine, for "Consciousness" and "The Black Martyr" by Rufus Irving Nickens, and "Poem" by Warrington Hudlin II.

Albert Young for "One"

The publisher has made diligent efforts to trace the ownership of all copyrighted material in this volume, and believes that all necessary permissions have been secured. If any errors have inadvertently been made, proper corrections will gladly be made in future editions.

In appreciation . . .

The poems in this anthology were selected with the help of dozens of persons across the country. Their faith in young people is evidenced by cartons of literary magazines and unpublished manuscripts which they gathered from young poets or urged them to submit on their own. Amassing this poetic treasure would not have been possible without the assistance of:

Terri Bush and June Jordan, Directors of The Voice of the Children, Inc., New York; Sheila Murphy, Teachers and Writers Collaborative, New York; Elaine Amidon, editorial advisor of *What's Happening?* New York; Philip Roy, editor, *Eclectic Magazine*, Philadelphia; William D. Boutwell and Lee Bennett Hopkins, Scholastic Magazines, Inc.; Gerald G. Jackson, Yale Summer High School; B. Jo Kinnick, Jean Wilson, Florence Miller, and Virginia Reid, Oakland Public Schools; Warren Doty, Simon Gratz High School, Philadephia; Miriam E. Peterson and Florence Gottschalk, Chicago Public Schools; Ruth Thomas, Milwaukee Public Schools; Ethel Richards, Public Schools of East Orange, N. J.; Carrie Robinson, Alabama State Department of Education; Robert Probst, Norfolk Public Schools; Charlotte Brooks, District of Columbia Public Schools; Myra Cohn Livingston, Beverly Hills, California; Lillian Morrison, New York Public Library; Olga N. Pobitsky, Detroit Public Library; Vilma M. Krusko, Cleveland Public Library; Jane Manthorne and Diane Farrell, Boston Public Library; Binnie

Tate, Los Angeles Public Library; Rowena M. Smith, Upward Bound Program, Hofstra University; Florence Howe, Goucher College; Glenn J. Christensen, Lehigh University; Charles E. Schaeffer, Fordham University.

As Gerald Jackson put it, "Somebody turned on a tap in these kids, and the poetry just kept coming."

Choosing from such a flood of poetry was not easy. My task was facilitated by several consultants to whom I am deeply indebted: William Stafford, poet, of Portland, Oregon; Binnie Tate, Young Adult Librarian of Los Angeles; Jean Wilkinson, high school teacher in Berkeley; Sonya Blackman, buyer for Books Unlimited in Berkeley; Florence Howe, Director of the Goucher Poetry Project in the Baltimore city schools; Deborah Stone, a former undergraduate participant in the Goucher Poetry Project; and my husband, Alexander L. Crosby, a steadfast friend of the young.

Their help has been invaluable, but I take full responsibility for the choice of poems and their arrangement in this volume.

NANCY LARRICK

Quakertown, Pennsylvania
March 1, 1970

I Heard a Scream in the Street is a selection of poems drawn from literally thousands written by children and young people who live in the city. The youngest contributor was in the fourth grade when he wrote his poem for this book; the oldest was eighteen and still in high school.

Many of these poems first appeared in school newspapers and literary magazines—a few of them slick publications with full-color illustrations, others crudely dittoed in bleary lavender ink. Some of the most striking poems have come from out-of-school writers' workshops and the underground student press where innovation and protest flourish.

Not all city poets write about the city, of course. But most of the young city writers are deeply concerned with the urban world that engulfs them, a world where streets are littered, neighbors are starving, and violence is normal.

N. L.

A Scream

Late one night
I heard a
Scream in the street.
When I went to look
There was no one
There.
Perhaps it was
The moon
Praying.

Allan Richards
Philadelphia, Pennsylvania

Contents

1

People Pushing
and Rushing

The City

The city is full of people
pushing and rushing for the check
the city is kids playing in the park
telling their mothers the hell with them

It's full of hate and war
with people never knowing who to turn to for help.
it's a prison with people fighting for freedom
Black white.
the city's full of them.

Juanita Bryant
New York, New York

Faces

An old man
Thrown into the street
And faces
A little boy
Crying for meat.
And faces
People
Fighting for the right
And faces
Children,
Crying in the night
And faces
Each face
With something to give,
But each face
Striving to live.

Shelley McCoy
East Orange, New Jersey

16

What's in the Newspaper Tonight?

I push through a crowd of unbelievers
Who cower together in their fright
I watch the pallid faces that prepare themselves
To ask "What's in the newspaper tonight?"

There are terror and bloodshed all over
And I see the stark reality of war
And the editors print letters from angry men
Who are galled by the unrest among the poor.

If you see a screaming face it doesn't matter
Whether it's black or white or yellow—blood is red
Though he "killed to save America" it's murder still
Death has no degrees—and now he too is dead.
and through it all the newsman stands
selling ruthlessly
grinning toothlessly.

Ron Holzinger
Haddonfield, New Jersey

The afternoon drags its feet more and more slowly
   across the clock face:
Someone up top figured out the five o'clock endurance
   point.
The dusk and dark break out the stars and some variant
   of moon,
And we crawl out like newly blossomed butterflies to fly
Among the lights and life. Somewhere, sometime, my
   love,
There is beauty and joy on the avenues.
Fly home. Drift home, Stay home. You live in a city.
A city with people. With anything. Doing all. And
   everything.
Run, child, run fast through the drifting flakes of white
   ash from Con Edison
To catch the last star
And live.

Carol Williams
Jamaica Plain, Massachusetts

Crowds on the train
Shoving, rushing
home to forget
All the pushing

Henry Gibau
New York, New York

One

"A cup of coffee for
me"
i notice a man; a stool away
BIG. (eating a platter—eggs, ham,
scrapple with a side order
of french fries)
his stomach reached across the
counter. he sits on one leg, afraid
to submit the weight
of both
to a single stool
PIG.
but in his coat pocket;
an anthology

Albert Young
Philadelphia, Pennsylvania

escaping the ghettos of New York
they trip
off they go into a paradise of
LSD, heroin, pot and speed
fantasy
the ecstasy of drugs

escaping the ghettos of New York
they drink
off they go into a paradise of
wine, beer, scotch, and gin
fantasy
the ecstasy of alcohol

to break through
only to return
yes, only to return to the
hell of an empty wine bottle
crushed beside the wall
in anger
no little drop left
to free a straining soul
to the hell of
an empty needle or a smoked down
red all dreams gone up
in smoke

escaping the ghettos of New York
they leave for a while
but they always always
return

Vanessa Howard
New York, New York

The hungry child roams the streets alone
He goes about and wishes he were home
He sits on a rock and cries, "Why do they let me die?"
He walks the streets with a sorrowful heart
He feels as if he is torn apart.

Vicky White
Oakland, California

Subway Ride on a Summer Day

The black and white of the posters
disappeared in a blur
as light became lighter.
The metal rolled louder
as airless became air
and tunnel became hill.

And as I looked out the window
I saw ivy climbing up an old chimney
and a little boy
walked across his stone and glass yard.

Debbie Solomon
Chicago, Illinois

on a wall
"Parmel and Jones"

directly near it
is a little boy no one sees

two strangers pass
staring at the sign on the wall

one say it's a vision
the second says it's a work of art

they call more people over
and all begin to awe

a bulldozer comes
"THE WALL IS BEING TORN DOWN," they scream

the two strangers fall in front of it
killing themselves to save the work of art

meanwhile the little boy no one sees
grabs his crayon
and draws on some other building.

Lawrence Fishberg
New York, New York

Hard But Soft

Six Negro boys with long black coats,
Old beat-up hats, sunglasses without lenses,
Cigarettes unlit, hanging out the side of their mouths,
Dragging their feet as they walk,
Knives in three hands,
Other three cursing.

Old woman,
Crossing the street,
Suddenly a car turns the corner at ten miles an hour,
Woman,
In the way;
Brakes won't work.

The boys run and try to get the lady out of the way,
But are too late.
Tears come rolling out.
Do such hard boys cry?
Yes,
For they are humans with emotions, too.

William Barbour, Jr.
New York, New York

The City is Burning
Holler, someone.
People run in the street
Police on the beat
Try to calm them down.

But the people panic
Buildings fall
The world is shaking

The people are ashes
With no wind to blow them away.

Henry A. Lewis
Oakland, California

What Is a City?

A city is the remembrance
of a gray rainy morning,
of gray carbon raincoats
and gray carbon people.

A city is a face picked out
of the crowd
a glint of recognition . . .

A city is a smoggy Tuesday afternoon,
the memories of a smoke-filled room
fading into the sound of a distant
police siren in the dark drizzle of dawn.

And sometimes when you've given up
a city is a renewed faith in humanity
Maybe only a smile
to make you believe again.

Mary Tobin
Jamaica Plain, Massachusetts

I Have No Fears . . .

Everyone
seems to be saying
how lonely
the city is.
To me
it is a paradise where
one can
talk and
laugh out loud and
stare at people . . .
I have no
fears in the
city;
for I believe that
man
is more gentle than
we think him
to be.
Outside
of all that smog
and fake confidences
lies
the true city . . .
full of love
and not afraid
of being
laughed at.

Joy Silverstein
Jamaica Plain, Massachusetts

2

Walk Down
My Street
and See

Walk Down My Street

Walk down my street
See who you meet
    Dirt and Dust
    Love and Lust
Heartaches live again   so die
People go to church
      Most of them lie
People talk to dogs   and have the fears of a child
       Act insane and get a police file
    What is it to me?
    Walk down my street and see.

Vincent Dorsett
New York, New York

Houses bent over look like
Old men who never will stand up
straight again.

Houses face to face
look like they are mad
at each other

Rickey McBride
Brooklyn, New York

love apple

tomato plants on the roof
had not been watered for two weeks
and they were dry to touch;
bent backwards
under their own weight,
sick and yellow.
But one plant,
all by itself, carried a red tomato,
fruit of neglect. Eaten,
it had the taste
of something sweet, poisonous.

Martha Scheiner
Philadelphia, Pennsylvania

Neighborhood

The quiet of the street in early morning
a silence of broken bottles,
perhaps a cat
the butcher's cat,
and windows
store fronts reflect store fronts
and the orange sun rising
over the edge of the curb.
A sudden siren cries
for those who die so early
and those who must live so late.
Behind the green window shades
and yellowing lace
beyond the potted plants
the neighbors lie sleeping.

Gwynne L. Isaacs
Philadelphia, Pennsylvania

Mainstream.
Flooded with wheels.
Polluted with exhaust fumes.
As if it were a cloudy day,
The misty fog
Rises from the thoroughfare.
So thick one can feel it.
Visibility is slight.
Foghorns shout
Fear,
Anger, and
Impatience.
Early in the morning
Just as the jewel-like dew
Is vanishing,
The air smells fresh and sweet
One can see for miles.
Then, chaos commences once again.

Cathy Magee
Norfolk, Virginia

A whirlwind: not of leaves that
grasp the sand and whirl it with them,
on a prairie;
but, of,
paper and cigarette butts,
on a sidewalk.

Charlotte Liberty Walker
New York, New York

beer cans
lie still
while the street light reflects
in the aluminum tops
surrounded by rocks
broken glass
and tiny bits of pebbles
the 65¢ wine bottle cries
the street is at a
star light star bright standstill
with the exception of the junkies
staggering
excepting the scent of Johnnie Walker
Sunset in Harlem.

Michael Goode
New York, New York

Ghetto

In the alley, trash scattered about,
paper, cans, furniture from the house,
   Old feathers from pillows rotten and mildewed
rank from age wet and damp.
   Sticks, rocks, broken pieces of glass,
leaves, car parts, weeds a foot high.
   Buildings with cracked paint, many standing
some nearly falling.
   Broken windows, cardboard tacked up
curtains in shreds, rooms too small.
   Plaster broken flattening on the floor, rain
dripping being caught by pots and pans
      clothes everywhere, bed unmade.
      dishes undone, floors untiled
      small gas stove to heat the house
      but it's home.

Roger Johnson
Oakland, California

You shout about freedom
Of going barefoot
But don't talk
About the broken bottles
And the damn dogshit.

Wilburt

New York, New York

The branches are broken the trees are brown and bare
The people dejected, in this neglected square.
Dogs couple undisturbed. The roots of trees,
Heave up the bricks in the sidewalk as they please.

Nobody collects the papers from the grass,
Or the dead matches, or the broken glass.
The elms are old and shabby: the people around
Stare lazily through paintless shutters at forgotten
     ground.

Linda Warren and Donna Dickson
Everett, Massachusetts

Scribbled on a once-clean wall,
Written by shallow minds,
Seeking kicks.
Obscene words,
Trash for the entertainment
of sophisticates;
Who stare
And laugh.
Amused.
Graffiti and verse,
For eyes interested in nothing.
Causing a sane man
to gaze and absorb.
He leaves,
Confused;
But happy,
and fulfilled to know that
John still loves Mary.

Paul Christensen
Chicago, Illinois

From my
window I see
ants crawling.
I see windows and
clotheslines. I see
red brick and cement.
From my window I see a
wall.

Alonzo Dunlap
New York, New York

Window; 3rd Story; 5th to the Right, Morning

Same damn city same damn window
Don't say it's raining
God it is a heavy rain
each drop seems to be pounding on my window
pleading for entrance
can't blame them
Seems you were pure a minute ago raindrop
before you began your descent that is
you'll have to adjust to survive in the city
take your chance with the others in the gutter
flow down the boulevard, being trampled
under foot if you're not swift
But even if you are
ending up in the same stinking sewer as the rest
to go into the stinking river
A stinking sea, then again
till you can't take any more
But you must!

Roger L. Drapeau, Jr.
Cambridge, Massachusetts

3

I Walk Through Crowded Streets . . . And Ask, "Who Am I?"

Who Am I?

I walk through crowded streets
Dirt and broken glass beneath my feet.
I gaze up at the crying red sky
And ask, "Who am I?"

Stella Mancillas
Los Angeles, California

Beneath the aging buildings
I stand alone
Against the elements of the wild city
With the ceilings of light bulbs
Breaking the darkness
Weakly
Far off.

Michael Deighan
Cleveland, Ohio

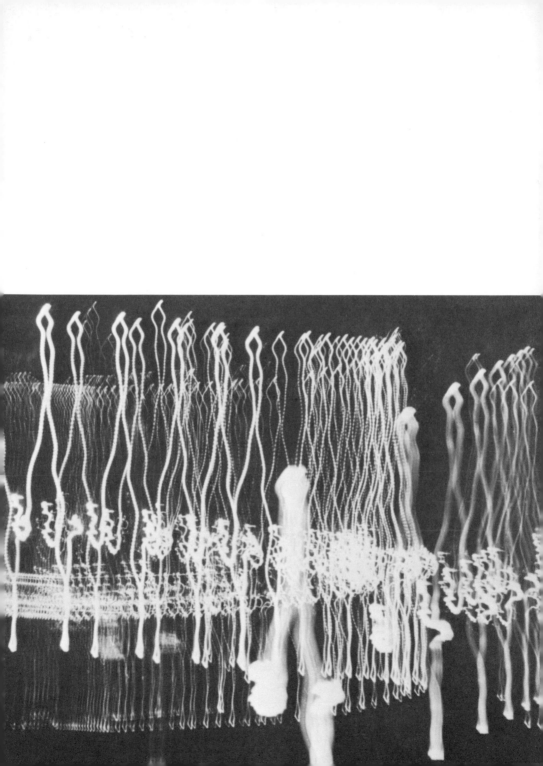

Summer in the City

Sitting doing nothing wanting to do something.
Waiting for someone that won't show up.
Walking and walking looking for something
not knowing what you're looking for.

Daniel McNally
New York, New York

The swings in the park
They are so lonely-looking
Until you play there

.

Cathleen McGlynn
Douglaston, New York

No One

I play alone
On the street
I try to talk
To everyone I meet
But still I'm lonely
As I sit on my stoop
In front of my house
I gaze at everyone
Passing by.
I am still lonely
I will not stay
This way very long
Thinking that I am
No one.

Barbara
New York, New York

i have friends
like staircases—
they wind and wind
with many, tiny narrow
steps
up and up
except they
always
stop at
just one room
at "their" top
and close
their door
tightly to all
others.

Cheryl Thornton
Oakland, California

Why Do They?

Why do they always let you walk by—
    not looking,
    not speaking,
    not caring?
Why do they always look the other way—
    not getting involved,
    not complicating matters,
    not leaving their world?
Why do they always wear a mask—
    not showing emotion,
    not showing desires,
    not showing themselves?
Why do they?
    Why
        do
           I?

Betty Wilkinson
Huntsville, Alabama

Alone

how
can i feel alone
while
i sit in the middle seat
in
the middle row on the school bus?
how
can i feel cold
while
i walk on burning pavement in
90-degree weather?
how
can i see black and white
while
i walk
in a flower garden?
how can i feel so sad
while all around beautiful things bloom
in the world?
how?

Mary Jane Hiers
Huntsville, Alabama

Have you ever loved at
night with the street lamp
in your face
or
with the sun shining
on your back?
Loving needs no special
time or place,
just so you love.

Aries Paige
Norfolk, Virginia

Poem

Money has its foot on my neck
It controls me.

I turn flips
Jump through hoops
And tell him what I think.

Every now and then
I even get applause

For being . . . all that reflect
        his thinking . . .
        his culture . . .
        his interest . . .

Maybe I should get his foot
Off my neck

But then . . .
I would have to stand.

Warrington Hudlin, II
East St. Louis, Illinois

I wanted badly to write
    something beautiful
But I've been straight too long
    And what used to be my mind is
    hung onto ugly images of a
    dry world.

No hope   no change
    How do you create when all
    around you dies and rots.

I wanted desperately to find
    some key, something that would be
    all-connecting and make us all one.
But I've been straight too long
    to listen to and follow an empty
    dream, while
    lying, always lying in order to live
    and grope numbly
    as the rest . . . . same
    as all the rest.

Oh, how I wanted to be right in my
    soul
But I've been straight too long
    and my doubts hide me
again

Neal Rosner
Chicago, Illinois

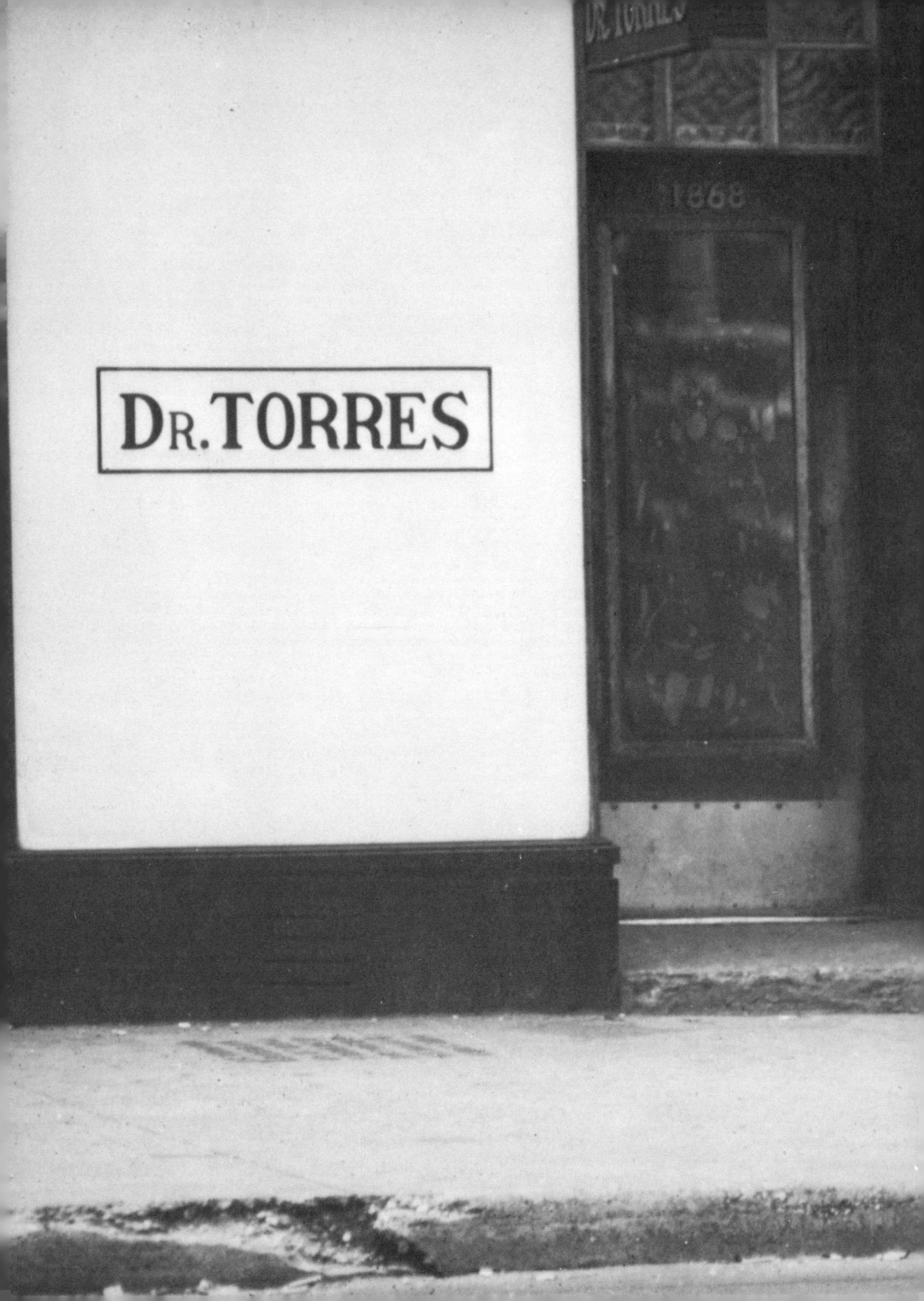
DR. TORRES
11868

And I've lived here all my lousy life
    but I don't cry about it.
And I've had to fight for dear life
    but I don't cry about it.

And I haven't seen all there is to see
Haven't learned all there is to learn
Haven't been loved like everyone
        should be,
But,
    but I don't cry about it.

    Only sometimes painfully
            dry, dry tears.

Lydia Martinez
New York, New York

What Now?

After tears
I lie on my bed
The cracks in my ceiling
Like so many children
Scattered
In summer streets
The walls
Grow
Ever closer
I cannot breathe.
Oh God! I don't want to die in Harlem.
Yet living here is hell
Even now
The sun is rising
On another day
Quick!—tell me
What now?

Lucia Martin
New York, New York

City Child

So maybe I have a
heart of
steel.
Something pulls me
to the city.
          (give me
     concrete meadows
     with neon flowers
     growing in the
     purple sunshine
     of vapor lights.
Something to satisfy my
steel soul)

Eileen McCormick
St. Louis, Missouri

I stand here against this lamp post
        looking at the ground.
Behind me is a whitewashed window,
        in front of me a street.
I stopped to think and rest, I don't really
        know why, I just got started
        and I'm not even tired,
        there is so much to do.
And yet, I stand here letting things catch up
        and go by.
I'm as close to the street as could be, yet
        I stand here disgusted and worn.
If I get out now, what then?
But, here I stand near this post
        between my past and my future
God damn it! I'm scared.

Ron Chafetz
Chicago, Illinois

The Generation Gap

And if I lied
and
said I did
would you respect me?

And if I damned
those I loved and who loved me
would you smile?

And if I saw thru your eyes
and
spoke with your words
would you believe me?

But I can't
and
you can't,
yet damn it, silence is no answer,

Listen,
Now.

Ellen Alexander
Chicago, Illinois

Walking past
small and dingy cafés,
I look in
and see
them all,
them with their long hair
their empty pockets
but worst of all
their empty heads full of all sorts
of screwy idealist ideas
that go nowhere.
And they sit there
trying to be so gone
    that man—
    They're so far gone
       they're lost!
And I?
I walk between them
among them
and cry right along with them
as I see myself in the dirty snow-water of the street.

Lydia Martinez
New York, New York

Me
Mean, hating
Running, talking, falling
Not liking anyone
Sad

Danny
New York, New York

4

I Dream
of Blackness

Why Do They Stare?

Why do they stare at me?
Is it because my clothes
Are torn and ragged?
Or is it because
My skin is dark and beautiful?
And they envy my beauty?
Why do they stare?

Wendy Rountree
East Orange, New Jersey

The Thoughts of a Child

I am a child.
But still I think,
I feel, I see
I hear, I wonder.
Why do they hate us so?
I see their sneers and jeers.
I hear them laugh and call us awful names.
Some of us are ashamed of being Black.
But I know this
I'm not ashamed of being Black
I'm proud; I will stand tall.
They *cannot* make me fall.

Denise Embry
Los Angeles, California

1960 — People walk the streets with black faces
       and straight hair
       In the night they put bleaching cream
       on their black faces
       Their skin is white but their
       features are black
       The whiter you are the better you are

1968 — People walk the streets with black faces
       and nappy hair
       They walk in the sun instead
       of hiding in the shades
       Their skin is black and their
       features are black
       Black is beautiful

Pauline Bird
New York, New York

Yes, I am a Negro.
Black as burnt ashes
Or white as the desert sands.
I am Unique!

No other one species on earth
Can be found in as many shades of color.

Yes, I am a Negro.
As much a man as can be found
But looked upon as mentally and
                    morally insufficient
I am underestimated!
One day I will prove to the
                    world my manhood
And be accepted as an equal son of God.

Yes I am a Negro.
Proud as the native Americans
Who fought the evils of "white progress"
I am rebellious!
No longer will I toil for another
No longer will I be ashamed of
                    my true African heritage

Yes, I am a Negro
Ambitious as any Caesar
Versatile as any Franklin
I am Beautiful!
And if asked on Judgment Day
             what I was on earth for
             was it for America?
I will quickly say
             No, I am a Negro.

John West
East Orange, New Jersey

Black is beautiful
Black is fine
Black is wonderful
Black is mine

*Graffito painted in brilliant colors on
an outside wall of the Highland Park
Free School, Roxbury, Massachusetts*

She came with lips of brown
to plant a kiss on all mankind
She came with arms ebony
black to soak the blood
of a bleeding war
She came with hair of deep black
to wash away the tears of sorrowing people
She loved them all, the least of all
of them she loved.

Betti Cox
Baltimore, Maryland

But I'm Still a Nigger

I goes to the white man's store
I buys the white man's clothes
I work in the white man's factories
But I'm still a nigger.

I spend the white man's money
I eat the white man's food
I play with the white man's daughter
But I'm still a nigger.

I learn in the white man's school
I eat in the white man's lunchroom
I go to war for the white man's cause,
"But I'm still a nigger, still a nigger."

Nathaniel
New York, New York

My Black Boy

Black boy, oh black boy,
What makes you tick
When white man near,

You play big and bold
Nowadays, but a long time
Ago you were too scared.

You say life is so damn
Hard, you say we can't get
Nowhere, well black boy,
Look where we at now!

Well now black boy you
Say white man ain't no
Good, you say white man
Can go to hell,

My black boy talk is so
Cheap, but if what you
Say is true, then why
the hell you marry a
White girl instead of me.

Carla J. Wade
Baltimore, Maryland

Mine

I want to walk the streets of a town,
Turn into any restaurant and sit down,
And be served the food of my choice,
And not be met by a hostile voice.
I want to live in the best hotel for a week,
Or go for a swim at a public beach.
I want to go to the best University
and not be met with violence or uncertainty.
I want the things my ancestors
thought we'd never have.
They are mine as a Negro, an American;
I shall have them or be dead.

Alice Jackson
Jackson, Mississippi

A Beautiful Black man
Sleeping in a corner
His mind wandering into the deepest of
Darkness
His suffering eyes closed
His mouth open wide as if he
Wants to eat up the White world
And spit it out into the hand
of the White man and then
wake up.

Charles Johnson
Oakland, California

Confusion.
this is
          a
Riot.
          (but don't you believe it)
I just shot my mother
          for the white man's
          Dollar.
I am blessed.
          It is predicted—
                    That I—
Will burn in Hell.
Black and Proud.
Death
          smells just
                    like
Life
          only sourer,
          (Where is *my*
               milk and honey.)

Rufus Irving Nickens
Houston, Texas

No Chains

Look!
No chains on my arms
No chains on my legs
No chains on them
can't you see?
But the chains on my mind are keeping
me from being FREE!

Howard Jones
Philadelphia, Pennsylvania

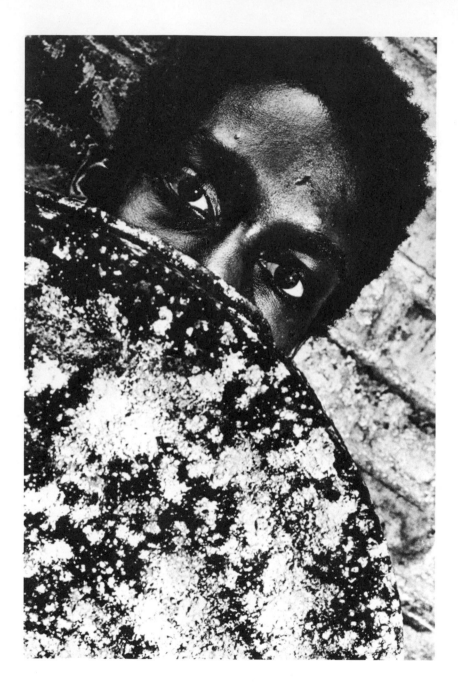

A Black Man's World

I seek the knowledge of a black man's world
The culture, the feelings of a black man's world
I've lived in the white man's world too long
For a hundred years and more
Separated by ghettos and slums
I long to be free to express myself
To express myself as a black man should
I long to write and tell of things
As only a black man could
I wish to be free
From society's bonds
Which keep me shackled to the white man's arm
I dream of blackness when weary at night
And see only whiteness when the day is bright
I seek the knowledge of a black man's world
The culture, the feeling of a black man's world.

Lorenza Loflin II
Milwaukee, Wisconsin

This is a Black Room
And all the people here are Black too.
There are windows on the wall,
But no one's gonna open them.

All the white people in the world
Are waiting outside this room,
And most of us don't want to look at them
Or hear them saying, "Shine my shoes, boy"
Or "Scrub my floor, woman."

I'm willing to open the window
To see if they've changed
But the Black people in this room might kill me.

Joshua Beasley
Baltimore, Maryland

Response to "This Is a Black Room"

Yes this is a Black Room
But all the people may not be truly Black.
And there may be more people than you think
Willing to open the window.

I know most Blacks don't want to see
or hear whites telling us to "shine their
shoes boy" or "scrub my floor woman" but
what can we do with no decent education
and people who always give up instead of
pushing on to glory?

Yes, brother this is a Black Room
and I think it is time to open
the window to look for a change
or this Black Room and the Black
people will die.

Deborah Dixon
Baltimore, Maryland

The Last Empty Seat

The white-skinned people are staring at you
But you don't feel bad; that's nothing new.
Just four seats are empty in the whole place,
And next to each one you study a face
That suddenly seems to avoid your eyes,
But that's O.K., it's no surprise.
As you pass rows A, B, C, and D,
You glance toward the first seat and you see
A woman awkwardly placing her hat
On the empty seat you're looking at.
Back in row H a fidgety hand
Is placed on another empty seat and
A mother shifts her sleeping baby
From her lap and onto the third seat. Maybe
You shouldn't have come. There's still one more
But you know you may's well walk out of the door
Right now. So you start to walk real fast
And you've reached the door when you glance at the
     last
Empty seat. And you hardly dare
To believe it. Nothing is there.

Richard Goodkin
Chicago, Illinois

I
WALK TALL MY BLACK CHILDREN
WALK TO THE FREEDOMS GATE
FOR THE BLACK CHILDREN
HOLD THE FORT
SEE HOW WELL THEY DO

II
TALK SOFT OF BEAUTY
BEAUTY THAT SHINES IN YOU
SPEAK OF LOVE NOT HATE
SPEAK OF FREEDOM NOT SLAVERY

III
FOR UNITY IS BEAUTIFUL
BUT BLACK BEAUTY IS FAR MORE BEAUTIFUL

IV
FOR THE WORLD CAN'T STOP YOU
STOP YOU FROM WALKING TALL
TO SPEAK OF TRUTH TO THE IGNORANT

V
WALK MY BLACK CHILDREN
WALK FOR ME, WHO CANNOT WALK
SPEAK FOR ME, WHO CANNOT SPEAK
SHOW THE WORLD HOW TALL YOU ALL STAND
FOR I AM PROUD OF MY BLACK CHILDREN

Sharón Boone
New York, New York

Consciousness

It's raining
    in New York.
I realized that
    just a moment
Ago.
(Funny)
It only took
    me about
5 seconds
    to see that.
It has taken
    me
Over 5 centuries
    to
Realize my place—
In the realm
    of Blackness.

Rufus Irving Nickens
Houston, Texas

5

I Am Frightened That the Flame of Hate Will Burn Me

SITTING UPON THE PICASSO KOALA BEAR STATUE THAT STANDS IN FRONT OF THE CIVIC CENTER BUILDING IN CHICAGO, ILLINOIS, THE CONVENTION CAPITAL OF THE WORLD

I sit here on top of this bear, eating cherries
I like cherries and log cabins
I also like Walnetoes and whipped cream and
walrus meat
I don't have any now because there is a hole
in my pocket
I look through my kaleidoscope glasses and I
see all sorts of thinnnnnnnnnnngs
I see peoples walking, thinking of themselves,
loving themselves and punching holes in IBM cards
with their teeth
I continue to look through my glasses and I
see more humans hating, sinning and rejecting cries
of help
I then put on my long-range adjustments and
focus them to a tenement on Taylor and Halsted
I see a little girl being eaten up by repulsive
retched rats
I take off my adjustments and I see peoples

laughing and neglecting and laughing and neglecting
So in disgust I get off this bear I'm sitting
on and, remembering to keep this city clean, I go
over to a trash can and vomit my ever lovin guts
out, cherry stems and all.

James Tomasello
Chicago, Illinois

Nature Poem

Across the river from Jersey comes the scent of pine
disinfectant, cleans out our nostrils with the keening

germ-killing activity of Ortho Benzyl Para Chloro Phenol
removes the nicotine stains from your lungs, the rust
from your veins and arteries. The stubborn stains
of guilt from your soul

The cool wind from Jersey mops across our faces
The scent of heavy-duty killing power.

George Meade
New York, New York

Zoo
(after hearing Simon & Garfunkel's recording "At the Zoo")

The lion bristles in his cage
As you go by with peanuts
For the elephants
The elephants
The elephants

The hippos lounge in murky depths
As you go by with smelly fish
For the polar bears
The polar bears
The polar bears

The parrots scream in stinky cages
As you go by with carrots
For the zebras
The zebras
The zebras

The ghettos cry with all their dirt
As we go by with food and money
For other countries
Other countries
Other countries

Anna Boorstin
Beverly Hills, California

kick a beer can in the stillness of the night
with whiplash and no flash or shining of a light
even lampposts stand still and cold
blown out dead and glass smashed in
and on the doors cruel and hard
beats the whiplash of the wind

I remember bare table no tablecloth
no crust of bread
I remember tired brothers and sisters
nowhere to sleep
six in a bed

I remember lights going out sometimes
and water always running cold
I remember sometimes standing bare
in outdoor shower ten years old

kick a bottle   look back on love
a penny-pinching God dwelling above
that bread from my mouth when
I was in need
Momma put all the money in church
with ten mouths to feed

I remember "nigger" and "bastard" and "boy"
I remember sadness and sometimes joy
I remember always "better luck next time"
and urinated hallways adorned with wine
tell me dear God in this heaven you dwell
if you don't feed me here
will they feed me in hell?
will my nights be warm?
and my money never low?
if it means a little comfort,
then Hell I must go.

kick a beer can in the street
watch a wino, junkie, bum
travel down God's damned concrete
odyssey of my home town slum.

Vanessa Howard
New York, New York

He said he had a dream.
A dream of peace and love and brotherhood.
And Chicago listened.
Cicero listened and spat in his eye.
The gangs listened and killed a fifteen-year-old boy.
The uneducated listened and bombed a school.
The ghetto listened and burnt, and bombed, and broke,
    and looted.
The mayor listened and said, "Shoot to kill."
Chicago didn't hear anything.

Arthur Alenik
Chicago, Illinois

126

Watch Dog

Big men walking around us with their guns and sticks.
Waiting for us to get out of line so they can hit us.
The pig says, "Go."
    every one starts to move away slow.

His stick lands a blow
    the man is dead
    and nothing will be said.

Tim Barnes
Oakland, California

Will the Wig Be Big Enough?

America, the land of money and huge dummies
Where everything costs double and there is plenty of
    trouble.
White at the top, black rock bottom
All kinds of flops we've got 'em
Slums and bums and skyscrapers
Rifles and guns and senatorial capers
Gorgeous poverty and filthy wealthy
Bombs stacked here and dropped over there
America, the land of the superior inferior
Cigarette cancer and banana smokers
LSD and the pill
Capital punishment and Mafia burial ground
Small cities big cities and no cities
Police bullies and teen-age crooks
Music and noise and silly toys
Banned books and the Johnson Birds
Polluted air and stupid laws
Rent and eviction and the charge-a-plate
A time for change but nobody with brains
Clean kids and gamin cousins
Commercials, divorce, and pigeon mess
Filled-up grain silos and empty stomachs
No place to die and no place to live
Big lies and small give

Burn the flag and make a new one
Integration on the vast plantation
The Indians are taking a stand as the Negroes band
Watch out Charlie, prepare to fight
Sampson had his hair cut but you are slowly going bald
America, can you afford a wig?

Peggy Crawford
Oakland, California

A War Game

A crippled soldier
returning from a menagerie
that the newspapers called
war

A crippled soldier
drinking away the bitterness
    of death
vomiting the sickness
    of uniformed murder

A crippled soldier
crying in hands
that spilled the blood
of children
    of laughing, weeping children
Even some children
that dressed up
in horrible suits,
with guns and bombs,
to play a fatally
unhappy game

Allan Richards
Philadelphia, Pennsylvania

Jail

You can lock me up in any jail.
Post me with no bail.
I would rather die in jail,
     burn in hell,
Than have to kill
     without my will.

Tim Barnes
Oakland, California

Haiku

JESUS STANDS AMONG
HELMETS, BULLETS, AND CLUBS
NAKED IN A GOLD LIGHT.

Reginald Lockett
Oakland, California

This Place

Take me away,
Away from this place
Let me get out of the Human Race.

Take me away
Far from this land, take me away
Where there is no man.

Take me away
Away from home
Where no one will care
What I do or what I own

Take me away
Away from disgrace
And let me get out of the Human Race.

Conrad Graves
New York, New York

i am frightened that
the flame of hate
will burn me
will scorch my pride
scar my heart
it will burn and i
cannot put it out.
i cannot call the fire department
and they cannot put out the fire within my soul
i am frightened that the flame
of hate will burn me
if it does
i will die

Vanessa Howard
New York, New York

Index of Poets and Titles

Index of First Lines

Index of Poets and Titles

Index of First Lines

Photographic Credits

All photographs reproduced in this book are prize winners from the annual Scholastic Magazines-Eastman Kodak Contest.

Jeffrey Barnett, New Rochelle, New York, page 52.

George Berke, Levittown, New York, pages, 33, 45.

Bruce Berman, Palm Springs, California, pages 118, 122.

James Carpenter, Erie, Pennsylvania, page 42.

Pedro Espinal, New York, New York, page 38.

Richard Frishman, Deerfield, Illinois, pages 65, 78-79.

Fred Kautsky, Cicero, Illinois, pages 30-31

Richard Kopstein, Bethpage, New York, pages 48-49.

Thomas Lippman, Pomfret, Connecticut, pages 2, 81.

Verna Miller, New York, New York, page 25.

Prince Nairn, Los Angeles, California, cover photograph and page 57.

Mark Packo, Oregon, Ohio, pages 98, 122.

Wolfgang Piegorsch, Hartsdale, New York, pages 14, 26, 35, 88.

Stephen Rawson, Swathmore, Pennsylvania, page 66.

Fred Schweitzer, New York, New York, page 108.

William Snell, San Francisco, California, pages 60, 69.

Barry Spritzer, New York, New York, pages 63, 84.

Harry Stalf, Cincinnati, Ohio, page 105.

Emily Wheeler, Fairfax, Virginia, pages 19, 73, 113.

Danny Yates, San Francisco, California, page 92.